WITHDRAWN
FROM THE RECORDS OF THE
MID-CONTINENT PUBLIC LIBRARY

Nature

Fold-Along Stories
Quick and Easy Origami Tales
About Plants and Animals

736.982 K126
Kallevig, Christine Petrell.
Nature fold-along stories

MID-CONTINENT PUBLIC LIBRARY
Raytown Branch
6131 Raytown Road
Raytown, MO 64133   **RT**

Text and Illustrations by

Christine Petrell Kallevig

International
P. O. Box 470505, Cleveland, Ohio 44147

D0451165

By the same author:

Folding Stories: Storytelling and Origami Together As One
Holiday Folding Stories: Storytelling and Origami Together
     For Holiday Fun
All About Pockets: Storytime Activities For Early Childhood
Bible Folding Stories: Old Testament Stories and
     Paperfolding Together As One
Carry Me Home Cuyahoga: A Children's Historical Novel
Fold-Along Stories: Quick and Easy Origami Tales for
     Beginners
Please Pass Grandma's Leg - AKA: The Case of the Sacked
     Potatoes
Our Sculptures Ourselves: A New Look at Public Art in
     Northeast Ohio

Copyright © 2009 by Christine Petrell Kallevig
All rights reserved. No part of this book may be reproduced or transmitted in any form or by any means, electronic or mechanical, including photocopying, recording, or by any information storage and retrieval system, without permission in writing from the Publisher.

Storytime Ink International
P. O. Box 470505,
Cleveland, Ohio 44147
Web site: storytimeink.home.att.net
Tel. (440) 838-4881
Fax (270) 573-4913
E Mail: storytimeink@att.net

ISBN 978-09628769-2-9

Illustrations by Christine Petrell Kallevig
Photographs by Christine Petrell Kallevig

First Edition
10 9 8 7 6 5 4 3 2 1
Printed in the United States of America
Library of Congress Control Number: 2008908734

MID-CONTINENT PUBLIC LIBRARY - QU

3 0003 00475947 6

MID-CONTINENT PUBLIC LIBRARY
Raytown Branch
6131 Raytown Road
Raytown, MO 64133

RT

To my special friends at Origami USA, the world's largest organization of origami enthusiasts: I am honored and humbled to have been selected as the recipient of the 2008 Florence Temko Award. My participation at the Origami USA conference inspired this new Storigami collection. Thank you for your kind support, positive encourgement and especially, your unwavering devotion to origami in all its various forms.

I would also like to express my gratitude to the many thousands of students, teachers, librarians, parents, and grandparents who have participated so enthusiastically in my paper folding sessions and storytelling programs since 1990. Thank you for your generosity and contagious energy. These nature stories are for you to enjoy and share with others.

How To Make The Origami Figures

1. Origami paper is available in a variety of lovely colors and textures, but all of the figures in this book can be made very satisfactorily with regular 20 lb. office paper, too. Experiment with different weights, but avoid soft papers that tear easily or resist folding.

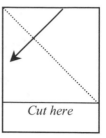

Cut here

2. Most origami figures start as squares, so each side must be exactly the same length. To cut a square from letter-sized paper, fold one corner down and trim away the excess. Save the leftover strip of paper for use in "Toadly Awesome" on page 69.

3. Use a hard, flat surface when making the initial folds on the prefolded model required for each story. Line up edges and corners precisely and hold in place before creasing. This sample model should be as large and as accurate as possible. Use stiff construction paper, freezer wrap, brown paper bags, gift-wrap, or art paper to make oversized models.

4. Follow each step in the order it is given.

5. Explanation of symbols:

   • Shaded areas indicate that the back side of the paper is now facing up.

   • Arrows point to the direction of the fold.

   • Broken lines indicate where the next fold will be. Unless specifically noted, dotted lines are "valley folds," where the resulting crease resembles an indented valley shape.

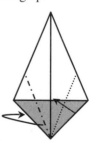

   • Solid lines mark an existing crease, fold, or edge.

   • Dots & dashes mean that the next step is a "mountain fold," where the edges align in the back of the figure and the resulting crease resembles a mountain.

   Flip the figure over to the reverse side.

   Rotate the figure.

   Push the corner into the inside of the figure.

   Fold and then unfold.

Table of Contents

Presentation Guidelines

1. **Select stories appropriate for your group** - Every story in this book features a different origami model. The tales can be enjoyed superficially by very young children or may be interpreted on deeper levels by older, more sophisticated listeners. Use the recommendations on each title page to gauge your group's readiness. The stories were designed as fold-along experiences, but it's perfectly acceptable to simply tell them without asking the audience to participate.

2. **Prefold the origami figure** - When creases are already made, the folding steps fall into place effortlessly and seamlessly, enabling attention to be focused on the needs of the listeners and the dynamics of the story. A flat surface to press against is not needed for refolding, so the large sample origami model can be held high for everyone to see. Even though the sample model does not require creasing as it's refolded, it's best to include the creasing motions anyway. Listeners imitate the presenter, and each of their steps must be thoroughly creased for best results.

3. **Be familiar with the story** - Practice refolding the origami model while reading the story aloud so that it's clear which actions or events are represented by the folding steps. Presenting with an open book is acceptable. Memorizing is not necessary.

4. **Establish structure by explaining the rules** - Before distributing paper, clearly announce what you want your listeners to do: copy your paper folding and if necessary, help each other. It's best not to stop and directly assist anyone during the story because it can create an undesirable avalanche of dependency and lead to the mistaken impression that origami is difficult. Instead, pause and repeat the folding step until everyone has copied you or has been helped by someone else. Offer reassurance that they can do it and that you're not in a hurry.

5. **Expect and accept imperfect first efforts** - Avoid criticizing lopsided or ragged first results. Instead, emphasize the folding sequence by referring to the progressive steps as they're labeled in the story. To increase quality, suggest making another origami model to share with a friend.

6. **Enhance the story with related activities** - Try some of the follow-up activities listed after every story. They're fun and reinforce learning.

Storytelling + Origami = Storigami

The concept is simple. While telling or reading a story, paper is folded into shapes that depict or illustrate an action, setting, or character. When the story ends, a surprise three-dimensional figure is created. The reader's or listener's mind automatically pairs the story events with the progressive folding steps, so while enjoying the story, an origami model is also learned.

Author Christine Petrell Kallevig has presented Storigami to the public steadily since 1990. This book, her fifth collection of origami stories, emerged from a blending of those performances with her favorite non-writing pastime, hiking, bicycling, camping, and canoeing in the great outdoors. What better way to express her love and respect for nature than to illustrate it with her other passion, origami, the ancient art of Japanese paper folding?

These nature-themed stories work well for people of all ages in large or small groups. They can also be enjoyed at home by single readers or families. The content is factual and provides basic information about biology and ecology. Success with these simple stories goes a long way toward conquering the irrational fear of origami that's still very prevalent in the general public today. There are also several educational benefits resulting from the combination of storytelling and origami:

➢ **Improved listening skills:** Paper folding adds interest and grabs attention. Listeners are curious and motivated to pay closer attention.

➢ **Opportunities to practice right cerebral hemisphere visualization skills:** Listeners and readers imagine the scenes described in the stories and understand the symbolic representations of the progressive origami folds. Researchers believe this ability is related to skills located in the right brain, an area sometimes overlooked in conventional learning tasks.

➢ **Opportunities to practice left cerebral hemisphere language comprehension skills:** Listeners and readers understand the words used in the stories. Language comprehension is a skill that is located primarily in the left-brain.

➢ **Emphasis is placed on multi-sensory, integrated whole-brain learning:** Visual, tactile, and auditory senses are all combined to provide the right and left cerebral hemispheres with input, resulting in an atmosphere of whole-brain learning. Learning is most effective when several areas of the brain are activated simultaneously.

➢ **Memory enhancement:** Short-term memory is improved through paired associations (story events with folding steps) and multi-sensory stimulation.

➢ **Improved fine motor skills:** Folding and manipulating paper provides practice in eye-hand coordination.

➢ **Opportunities to examine and practice spatial relationships:** Spatial concepts include right and left, front and back, top and bottom, inside and outside, beside, under, parallel, symmetrical, etc. These are all key elements of origami.

➢ **Supplemental material:** The index lists optional follow-up activities in math, language arts, social studies, art, and science.

➢ **Opportunities to enhance creativity and social skills:** Increased self-esteem is a by-product of successfully learning new skills and new experiences generate new ideas.

Who Benefits From Nature Fold-Along Stories?

➢ Children and their parents or grandparents who want to build family traditions or participate together in a fun and creative new hobby.

➢ Art teachers or origami specialists who need an effective and non-threatening method to teach origami to beginners.

➢ Science teachers and librarians who want to reinforce learning about plants, animals, and the environment.

➢ Recreation, troop, and club leaders who organize and present nature-themed activities on limited budgets.

➢ Camp leaders, storytellers, or nature programmers who serve families or groups composed of mixed ages, multiple interests, or widely diverse ability levels.

This seagull is easy to fold, but will it fly?

About the story: Λ food chain, from mosquitos to seagulls and back again, is described and illustrated with sequential origami folds.

Recommended ages:
   Listening only: All ages.
   Listening & paper folding: age 5 – adult.

Required materials: Prefold the bird from a large square, and then completely unfold it for storytelling. Paper with contrasting sides creates the best results.

Special notes:
   1. Several folds in this design are estimates and can vary in depth from other folders, but paired folds should be symmetrical within the model itself.
   2. The fold in Step #4 is a mountain fold. Make sure it's folded toward the back of the model.

Pain and Gain of Nature's Food Chain

What are you more afraid of, a grizzly bear or a mosquito? Your answer will probably depend on where you are, right? If you're in the Alaskan Wilderness and a 500-pound grizzly bear wants to eat you, then it's definitely scarier than a tiny, six-legged, two-winged insect that only wants to eat *part* of you. But if you're just about anywhere else in the world, the best answer might be a mosquito the size of a grizzly bear!

Did you know that mosquitos have killed more people than all other insects and animals combined? There are about 3,000 different kinds in the world. Some, not *all,* mosquitos spread deadly diseases when they bite people and animals. Female mosquitos only bite when they need blood to make eggs that they deposit into fresh water, like **lakes** *(hold up the square to represent a lake)* or **rivers.** *(Demonstrate with Step #1.)*

If the temperature of the water is warm enough, mosquito eggs quickly hatch into larvae, which are a favorite meal for helpful creatures like dragonflies and **small fish**. *(Demonstrate with Step #2.)*

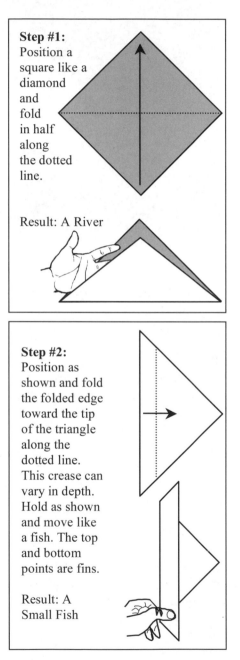

Step #1:
Position a square like a diamond and fold in half along the dotted line.

Result: A River

Step #2:
Position as shown and fold the folded edge toward the tip of the triangle along the dotted line. This crease can vary in depth. Hold as shown and move like a fish. The top and bottom points are fins.

Result: A Small Fish

Small fish are often eaten by **bigger fish** *(demonstrate with Step #3)*

…which are in turn eaten by other animals, like this **fox.** He's an omnivore and will eat almost anything he can get hold of. *(Demonstrate with Step #4.)*

After the fox gobbles **down** *(demonstrate with Step #5)* some of the fish, a **seagull** arrives to clean up the rest. *(Demonstrate with Step #6, and then completely unfold the seagull. Refold it quickly as you review each step of the food chain.)*

Then the seagull is bitten by a female mosquito so she can lay her eggs in **lakes and rivers**, the eggs hatch into larvae which are eaten by **small fish**, which are eaten by **bigger fish**, which are caught by **foxes,** partly gobbled **down,** and finally finished by **seagulls**, who are bitten by female mosquitos - and on and on it goes, the pain and gain of nature's food chain.

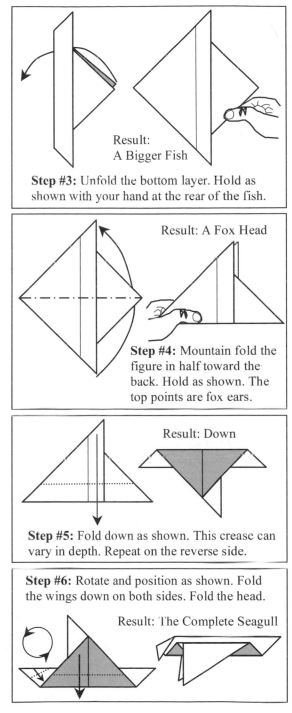

Result: A Bigger Fish

Step #3: Unfold the bottom layer. Hold as shown with your hand at the rear of the fish.

Result: A Fox Head

Step #4: Mountain fold the figure in half toward the back. Hold as shown. The top points are fox ears.

Result: Down

Step #5: Fold down as shown. This crease can vary in depth. Repeat on the reverse side.

Step #6: Rotate and position as shown. Fold the wings down on both sides. Fold the head.

Result: The Complete Seagull

Optional Follow-Up Activities

1. Fold more seagulls with increasingly smaller squares of paper, making sure to label each step with its name from the story. Pairing story events with folding steps greatly enhances short-term memory of both, and using ever smaller paper increases precision.

2. What other origami plants and animals featured in this book form a circular food chain? Fold them, arrange them in order, and display on a bulletin board or suspend as a three-dimensional mobile.

3. Will the seagull fly? Not very well. It needs some modifications. Experiment with changing the angle of the wings and collapsing the head to the inside of the figure. Make a new bird with fresh, unfolded paper. Try to glide each step as you build it. Does the plain triangle in the first step glide better than the finished seagull? Compare and contrast the flying results of birds made from differently textured or sized papers. Does heavier, thicker paper result in longer flights? Do miniature birds fly further?

4. Research the actual colors and markings of different species of birds, and then draw these characteristics on the origami model. Attach a short summary about the featured bird. Include its scientific name and facts about its habitat, diet, and size.

5. Several fables, legends, and folktales feature foxes as prominent characters. Identify as many as you can. Do the stories share similar themes or plots? Is the fox always a scoundrel? Write your own story about your origami fox. Make it fanciful, factual, or both!

6. Find and build other origami birds. Make a display showing the various styles and instructions. Compare the number of folding steps and levels of difficulty.

7. Use this story to introduce or complement discussions about:
   a. Habitats and characteristics of mosquitos.
   b. Nature's food chain. Is it cruel? Why or why not?
   c. Are there really mosquito fish? Where do they live?
   d. What diseases do mosquitos carry? Who is vulnerable?
   e. Grizzly bears. What is their position in the food chain?

Fold this traditional cicada with paper that has contrasting sides.

About the story: Prime numbers are demonstrated with progressive origami folds.

Recommended ages:
Listening only: All ages.
Listening & paper folding: age 5 – adult.

Required materials: Presenters should prefold the cicada from a large square, and then completely unfold it for storytelling. Paper with contrasting sides creates the best results.

Special notes:
1. This cicada is often one of the first models that beginning paper folders learn to make.
2. The counting sequences in the story are only suggestions and may be adjusted for individual presentation styles.
3. The depth of the resulting fold in Steps #4 and #5 can vary between different folders.

Prime Time

Prime numbers are very interesting to mathematicians and scientists, especially when they appear mysteriously in nature. Prime numbers are easy to remember. They are whole numbers that can only be divided by themselves and the number one.

For example, **two** is a prime number. When we divide these two halves by two, we get one whole square. *(Hold up a square and point to each of its halves.)*

Three is a prime number, too. *(Demonstrate with Step #1. Point to the three corners to represent the number three.)*

But **four** is not prime. It can be evenly divided by 2. *(Demonstrate with Step #2. Point to and count out the four corners of the resulting diamond shape. Continue pointing and counting in the same way for all the next numbers, too.)*

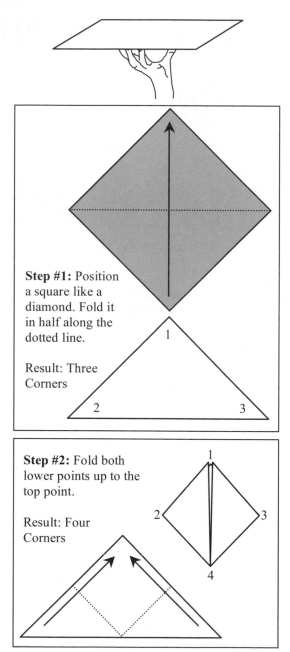

Step #1: Position a square like a diamond. Fold it in half along the dotted line.

Result: Three Corners

Step #2: Fold both lower points up to the top point.

Result: Four Corners

Five is prime, *(demonstrate with the first part of Step #3)* ...but **six** is not. *(Demonstrate with the next part of Step #3.)*

Seven is a prime number *(demonstrate with Step #4)* ...and so is **eleven**. *(Demonstrate with Step #5.)*

The next prime numbers, 13 and 17, are especially important to this insect, the **periodical cicada.** *(Demonstrate with Step #6.)*

Periodical cicadas, also called Magicicadas, are nature's loudest insects. They develop underground for 13 years in hot regions and for 17 years in cooler areas. Millions emerge at the same time in huge groups called broods.

They climb up to the treetops where they drink sap, mate, lay eggs, and then die after only 30 to 40 days. A few weeks later, billions of cicada babies called nymphs fall to the ground and burrow down two to 18 inches until they latch unto a tree root for the next 13 or 17 years. Why are they associated with these prime numbers? No one knows for sure. It's a prime unsolved mystery of nature.

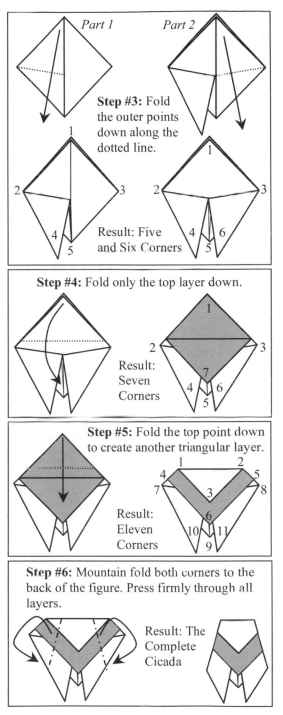

Part 1   Part 2

Step #3: Fold the outer points down along the dotted line.

Result: Five and Six Corners

Step #4: Fold only the top layer down.

Result: Seven Corners

Step #5: Fold the top point down to create another triangular layer.

Result: Eleven Corners

Step #6: Mountain fold both corners to the back of the figure. Press firmly through all layers.

Result: The Complete Cicada

Optional Follow-Up Activities

1. Fold more cicadas with increasingly smaller squares of paper, making sure to label each step with its name from the story. Pairing story events with folding steps greatly enhances short-term memory of both, and using ever smaller paper increases precision.

2. Add cicada eyes by folding each corner down and back up again. Finish by folding the little point in the middle to the back.

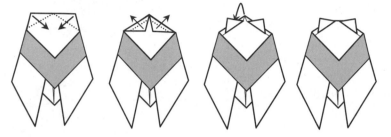

3. Research when the next broods of periodical cicadas are due to emerge. Make a timeline for your region. Compare it to the emergence schedule of other areas. Remember, not all cicadas are periodical. Some species stay underground for much shorter lengths of time.

4. People and animals regularly eat some insects. Find cicada recipes and write them on the back of the origami cicadas to distribute during the next emergence in your area.

5. Use the cicadas as nametags, bulletin board decorations, ornaments, place marks, or lace with yarn for necklaces. Glue tiny cicadas onto earring posts or string several together like beaded jewelry.

6. Make a chart of all the prime numbers from 2 to 101.

7. Use this story to introduce or complement discussions about:
   a. Habitats and characteristics of insects. Why are cicadas special?
   b. Prime numbers. Where else do they occur in nature?
   c. The history, discovery, and study of prime numbers.
   d. Do cicadas damage trees or wildlife?
   e. Locusts. Are the same insect as cicadas?

Two snakes can be folded from one letter-sized piece of paper.

About the story: Origami folds illustrate a watchful visit to a popular riverside park.

Recommended ages:
　　Listening only: All ages.
　　Listening & paper folding: age 6 – adult.

Required materials: Presenters should prefold a snake from a large strip that's approximately 2.5 times longer than its width, and then completely unfold it for storytelling. Paper with contrasting sides creates the best results.

Special notes:
1. This snake is simple, but bulky. Press firmly through all layers for the final fold.
2. Pinch one end to add a head. Hold by the tail and jiggle the figure as through it's trying to slither away.

River Watch

Not far from here, bicyclists, hikers, and boaters love to visit a scenic riverside park. *(Demonstrate with Step #1.)*

Upriver *(demonstrate with the top corners of Step #2)* and **downriver,** *(demonstrate with the lower corners of Step #2)* people in brightly colored canoes, rafts, and **kayaks** float with the current or paddle hard against it. *(Demonstrate with Step #3.)*

If we look carefully, we can see several narrow, deep holes dug into the ground beneath the **tall grass** and shrubs that rise away from the water. *(Use the reverse side of the kayak to represent a tall blade of grass.)*

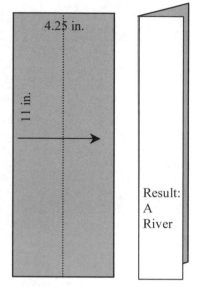

4.25 in.

11 in.

Result:
A
River

Step #1: Fold the paper in half.

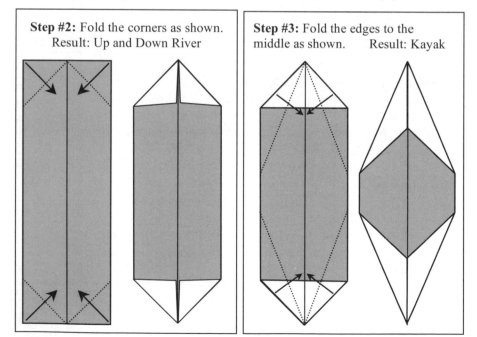

Step #2: Fold the corners as shown. Result: Up and Down River

Step #3: Fold the edges to the middle as shown.   Result: Kayak

Curious, we stand still and study the riverbank. Finally we notice a slight movement in the grass, and near the ground, we see the glint of **beady rodent eyes** staring up at us. *(Demonstrate with Step #4.)*

Then instantly, in just a **blink of an eye,** *(demonstrate with Step #5)* the little creature scampers away and disappears into one of the deep, dark holes.

That's when this tongue-flicking reptile slithers across the trail and pauses nearby in a patch of sunlight. *(Demonstrate with Step #6.)*

Unlike the warm-blooded rodent that just escaped, a snake has to move between sun and shade in order to regulate its body temperature. It picks up odors and sound waves with its forked tongue, so this snake is tasting the air as it warms itself. It's taking in the river scene, just as we are.

Waiting, watching, and wondering what will happen next.

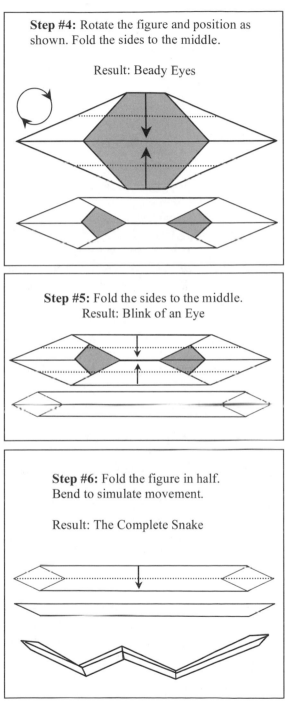

Step #4: Rotate the figure and position as shown. Fold the sides to the middle.

Result: Beady Eyes

Step #5: Fold the sides to the middle.
Result: Blink of an Eye

Step #6: Fold the figure in half. Bend to simulate movement.

Result: The Complete Snake

19

Optional Follow-Up Activities

1. Fold more snakes with increasingly smaller strips of paper, making sure to label each step with its name from the story. Pairing story events with folding steps greatly enhances short-term memory of both, and using ever smaller paper increases precision.

2. Try folding the snake from a dollar bill.

3. Sponsor a Forked Tongue Liars Contest. Write an opening phrase on several origami snakes and place them in a bag. Each person pulls one out, reads it, and then immediately begins to tell a one-minute tall tale. Record each whopper with a video camera. Award one point for every adjective and adverb that's used correctly. Deduct a point for each meaningless word, such as: "you know" "like" and "um." Give five bonus points for using only complete sentences. Make Forked Tongue medals for winners. Here's a few statements to get you started:

    a. Yesterday after school, a huge…
    b. You might not believe this, but
    c. No one knows this about me, but...
    d. I jump so…
    e. I run so…
    f. My desk is so…
    g. Under my bed, there are 1000…
    h. Lunch was so…
    i. This morning on the way to school, a tiny…

4. Research the actual colors and markings of different species of snakes, and then draw these characteristics on the origami model. Attach a short summary about the featured reptile. Include its scientific name and facts about its habitat, diet, and size.

5. Use this story to introduce or complement discussions about:
    a. Habitats and characteristics of reptiles.
    b. Rodents and other small mammals that live in holes.
    c. The ecology of rivers.
    d. Kayaking, rafting, and canoeing.
    e. Procedures for effective nature watching.
    f. Proverbs, folklore, or idioms about serpents and snakes.

Choose paper with contrasting sides when you make this owl.

About the story: Common characteristics of birds are described and illustrated by origami folds.

Recommended ages:
Listening only: All ages.
Listening & paper folding: age 6 – adult.

Required materials: Presenters should be prepared with a wide-tipped black marker. Prefold an owl from a large square, and then completely unfold it for storytelling. Paper with contrasting sides creates the best results. Do not draw the circles in Step #4 until you tell the story.

Special notes:
1. Repeat the valley fold on the reverse side for both Steps #2 and #3.
2. The fold in Step #5 is below the diagonal midline.
3. Strigiformes is pronounced: strij-eh-FOR-meez (the first syllable rhymes with fridge.)

A World of Birds

Wild birds live on every continent on Earth. Even though they have an amazing variety of shapes, sizes, colors, and behaviors, they all have a few things in common, too. Did you know that all birds, from the largest eagles to the tiniest hummingbirds, all have **beaks?** *(Demonstrate with Step #1. Open and close the paper to simulate a beak.)*

Another thing that all birds have is **wings**. *(Demonstrate with Step #2.)*

Not all birds use their wings to fly. *(Hold one end and gently wave the model so that the wings flap.)* Wings are useful for swimming or grabbing things, too.

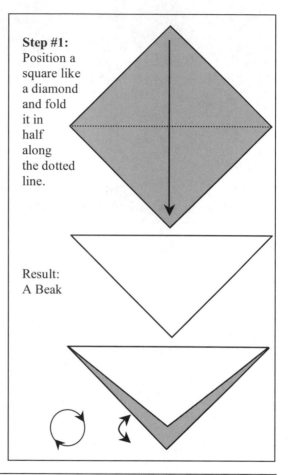

Step #1: Position a square like a diamond and fold it in half along the dotted line.

Result: A Beak

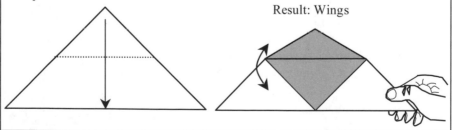

Step #2: Position as shown. Fold only the top layer down to the bottom edge. Repeat on the reverse side.

Result: Wings

And of course, all birds have **feathers.**

(Demonstrate with Step #3. Hold the figure at one end, tilt it slightly, and allow the model to separate slightly to resemble a feather.)

Not only do bird species look and act differently, they also live in a wide variety of places. Some birds live in **caves.**

(Unfold everything and draw two round circles to represent caves as shown in Step #4.)

Some live on the flat tops of mountainous regions, called **mesas.**

(Demonstrate with Step #4. Run a finger along the top edge to emphasize the mesa.)

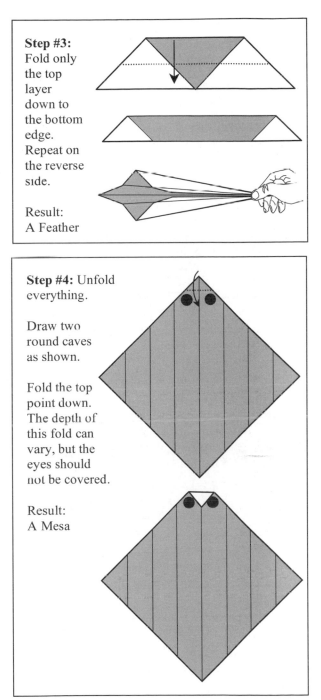

Step #3: Fold only the top layer down to the bottom edge. Repeat on the reverse side.

Result: A Feather

Step #4: Unfold everything.

Draw two round caves as shown.

Fold the top point down. The depth of this fold can vary, but the eyes should not be covered.

Result: A Mesa

23

Other birds live in **canyons or steep river valleys.** *(Demonstrate by putting a hand inside Step #5.)*

Birds live in every other type of habitat you can think of, such as...

(Ask the audience to name more habitats or keep reading the ones listed here.)

...jungles, forests, prairies, deserts, seashores, frozen icecaps, cities, and plain old hilltops. *(Point to the triangular shape of the figure.)*

Birds in the order of Strigiformes have learned to live everywhere except Antarctica. They're known for their sharp **beak...**

(Demonstrate with Step #6. Begin shaping the final creases in Step #7 as you talk about owls' other special characteristics.)

...excellent vision and hearing, powerful talons, and the ability to fly silently, especially at night. Whoo whoo whoo do you think I'm talking about?

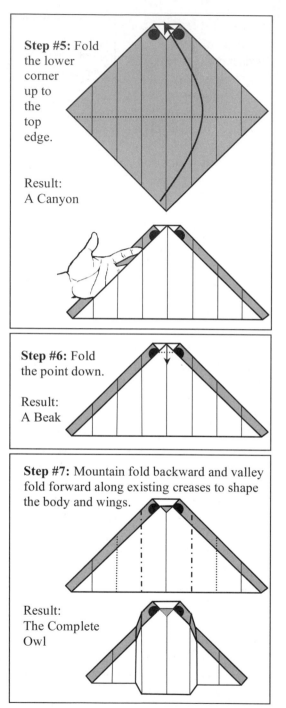

Step #5: Fold the lower corner up to the top edge.

Result:
A Canyon

Step #6: Fold the point down.

Result:
A Beak

Step #7: Mountain fold backward and valley fold forward along existing creases to shape the body and wings.

Result:
The Complete Owl

Optional Follow-Up Activities

1. Fold more owls with increasingly smaller squares of paper, making sure to label each step with its name from the story. Pairing story events with folding steps greatly enhances short-term memory of both, and using ever smaller paper increases precision.

2. This origami owl has a large flat area on its chest that works well as a frame for pictures, brief stories, or poems. The owl frames can be attached to a bulletin board or arranged as a freestanding display on a table or shelf.

3. Owls represent many different things to people worldwide. Research owl mythology. Make several origami owls and label them with each symbol you find. For example, owls represented wisdom in ancient Greece.

4. Research the actual colors and markings of different species of owls, and then draw those characteristics on the origami model. Attach a short summary about the featured owl. Include its scientific name and facts about its habitat, diet, and size.

5. Test your knowledge of owls by answering true or false to these statements. Answers are on the next page.
   a. Owls chew their food with 28 teeth.
   b. Owls are most active at night.
   c. Owls eat berries, seeds, and honey from beehives.
   d. Owls don't hear as well as bald eagles.
   e. Owls have big eyes in order to look scary at Halloween.
   f. Owls can turn their heads around in a complete circle.
   g. Owls use their sharp beaks to catch prey.
   h. Owls with feathery tufts on top of their heads are king owls.
   i. Owls have special feathers to help them fly silently.
   j. Owls have two legs and eight ticklish toes.
   k. Owls can only give a hoot.
   l. Only queen owls lay eggs.
   m. Owls are protected in the United States.
   n. Owls and witches are best friends.

6. Answers to the quiz:
   a. False, birds don't have teeth. Owls swallow their food whole or shred it into smaller pieces before swallowing.
   b. True, owls are nocturnal, but some hunt during the day, too.
   c. False, owls are birds of prey. They eat other birds, small mammals, insects, and reptiles.
   d. False, owls hear the best of all birds of prey.
   e. False, owls have big round eyes to improve their night vision.
   f. False, owls can only rotate their heads three-fourths of the way around.
   g. False, owls and other birds of prey hunt with the powerful talons on their feet.
   h. False, feathery tufts are decorations, not crowns.
   i. True, owls can swoop down and grab dinner without a sound.
   j. True, all eight owl toes are very strong and very sensitive.
   k. False, owls screech, hiss, and scream, too.
   l. False, all adult female owls build nests and lay eggs.
   m. True, it's illegal to capture or kill an owl.
   n. True, but only in fairy tales. Many years ago, owls represented evil or misfortune in some ancient superstitions.

7. Experiment with variously textured papers, including wallpaper, freezer wrap, construction paper, wrapping paper, and foil. What type of paper works the best?

8. Use this story to introduce or complement discussions about:
   a. Birds and their habitats and characteristics.
   b. Owls versus the forestry industry. Who wins?
   c. Greek roots of scientific words.
   d. Do owls migrate like other birds?
   e. Native American folklore has many references to owls. Compare and contrast some of the stories.

Add these leaves to origami flowers to make a full bouquet.

About the story: Photosynthesis in leaves is described and illustrated by origami folds.

Recommended ages:
Listening only: All ages.
Listening & paper folding: age 6 – adult.

Required materials: Presenters should prefold a leaf from a large square, and then completely unfold it for storytelling.

Special notes:
1. The width of the fold in Step #4 can vary between folders, but it should remain consistent for the rest of the pleating steps.
2. Leaf veins angle upward from the leaf midline in nature, so make sure that your fold lines branch outward and upward.

The Secret Life of Leaves

As we admire **mountains** *(demonstrate with Step #1)* blanketed with green-topped trees, we don't usually think about the individual leaves on those trees. There are so many, it's impossible to focus our eyes on just one or two. Leaves blur together into fanciful shapes, like the animals we imagine in puffy clouds or the craggy faces that frown down at us from steep stone ledges.

Leaves never look like they're doing anything amazing or important. They don't look like they're doing anything at all. Even though we can't see how they're doing it, leaves are actually very busy cleaning the air and making food for the plant they're attached to. Leaves make food for us, too, when we eat parts of plants, like fruits and vegetables.

Most leaves have two parts: a **stalk** that's connected to the growing stem of a plant, and a **blade** that's normally green because it contains chlorophyll. *(Demonstrate with Step #2. The area below the vertical midline represents the stalk and the rest of the model represents the blade.)*

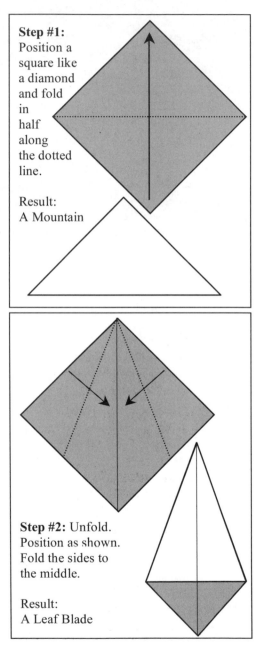

Step #1: Position a square like a diamond and fold in half along the dotted line.

Result: A Mountain

Step #2: Unfold. Position as shown. Fold the sides to the middle.

Result: A Leaf Blade

Leaf blades have two layers, the waterproof **upper epidermis** *(flip the model over to the smooth side)* and the more porous **lower epidermis** *(flip the model over to the first side)* where air goes in and out through tiny openings called stomata.

When **sunlight** *(demonstrate with Step #3)* shines on leaves, the green chlorophyll makes food by combining water carried from the roots with carbon dioxide let in through the stomata. This is called photosynthesis.

The food is carried from the leaves into the **stem...**

(Demonstrate with Step #4.)

...down into the roots...

(Demonstrate with Step #5.)

...and back up...

(Demonstrate with Step #6)

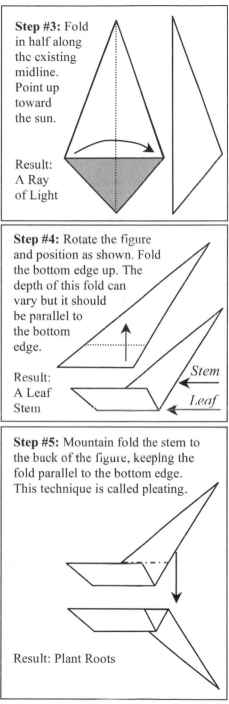

Step #3: Fold in half along the existing midline. Point up toward the sun.

Result: A Ray of Light

Step #4: Rotate the figure and position as shown. Fold the bottom edge up. The depth of this fold can vary but it should be parallel to the bottom edge.

Result: A Leaf Stem

Stem

Leaf

Step #5: Mountain fold the stem to the back of the figure, keeping the fold parallel to the bottom edge. This technique is called pleating.

Result: Plant Roots

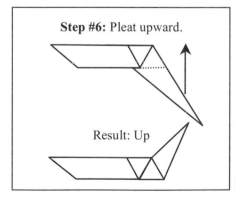

Step #6: Pleat upward.

Result: Up

...to the very **tip** of the whole plant...

(Demonstrate with Step #7.)

...through tubes called **veins.**

(Demonstrate with Step #8. Unfold the model to Step #2 to reveal the finished leaf with veins.)

Leaves have many colors,
    shapes, and sizes;
They change dramatically in
    the fall.
But photosynthesis in
    chlorophyll
Is the most amazing leaf fact
    of them all.

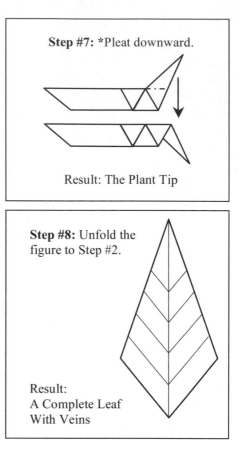

Step #7: *Pleat downward.

Result: The Plant Tip

Step #8: Unfold the figure to Step #2.

Result:
A Complete Leaf
With Veins

*Another way to illustrate pleating is to show all the valley and mountain folds together like this.

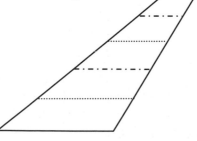

Optional Follow-Up Activities

1   Fold more leaves with increasingly smaller squares of paper, making sure to label each step with its name from the story. Pairing story events with folding steps greatly enhances short-term memory of both, and using ever smaller paper increases precision.

2   Experiment with variously textured papers and starched fabric, including wallpaper, freezer wrap, construction paper, wrapping paper, foil, cotton, and linen. Make a bouquet of leaves folded from different materials.

3.   Many poems have been written about leaves, flowers, and trees. Find some and compare and contrast the adjectives the authors used to describe plants. Write your own poem and copy it onto an origami leaf. Display several leaves as a tree of poems.

4.   Research the actual colors and markings of different species of plants, and then draw these characteristics on the origami leaf. Attach a short summary about the featured plant. Include its scientific name and facts about its habitat, diet, and size.

5.   Test your knowledge of plants by answering true or false to these statements. Answers are on the next page.
    a.   Water+Carbon Dioxide +Light+Chlorophyll=Photosynthesis.
    b.   Photosynthesis in leaves feeds all living things on Earth.
    c.   Plants get most of their water from roots.
    d.   Only green leaves have chlorophyll.
    e.   Blades of grass don't have enough room for photosynthesis.
    f.   Plants sleep at night.
    g.   Cacti don't have leaves so they must not be plants.
    h.   Botany is an abbreviation for a commonly asked question in malls, as in, "Have you bought any good books, lately?"
    i.   Autumn color change is caused by lack of water in the leaf.
    j.   Jack's beanstalk is the world's tallest living organism.
    k.   If people stopped exhaling carbon dioxide, plants would die.
    l.   Everyone gets a rash from touching poison ivy leaves.
    m.   25% of all medicines come from plants.
    n.   Some vengeful plants eat insects to get back at the bug world for damaging so many plants.

31

6. Answers to the quiz:
   a. True, as plants convert light to food, they also release the oxygen we need to breathe.
   b. True, photosynthesis results in a sugar called glucose that is stored in the plant. It's the basic source of energy for all plants and animals.
   c. True, plant roots have cells that absorb and store water for the whole plant.
   d. False, chlorophyll in ornamental purple or red leaves is hidden by the other pigments. If a plant is growing, it has chlorophyll.
   e. False, unless grass is mowed too short, lawns continue to photosynthesize as long as they are green.
   f. True, plants cannot make food without light so stomata close at night, causing leaves to droop.
   g. False, cacti do have tiny leaves, but they do most of their photosynthesis in stems.
   h. False, botany is the study of plants, not purchases.
   i. True, when veins stop transporting water through the leaf, green chlorophyll dries up and allows other leaf pigments to show.
   j. False, California Coastal Redwoods are taller (and real).
   k. False, people need plants for oxygen but plants do not need people for carbon dioxide.
   l. False, only 50% of people are bothered by poison ivy.
   m. True, one out of four medicines is made from plants.
   n. False, plants are peaceful. They only eat bugs in order to get nutrients they can't get from the soil.

7. Use this story to introduce or complement discussions about:
   a. Plants and their habitats and characteristics.
   b. Carbon dioxide and its impact on the planet.
   c. Greek roots of scientific words.
   d. Photosynthesis and its place in the planet's food chain.
   e. Different shapes, colors, and textures of leaves.

This cute coyote puppet is entertaining and easy to make.

About the story: Wild animals lose their natural habitat so they're forced to adapt to city living.

Recommended ages:
Listening only: All ages.
Listening & paper folding: age 7 – adult.

Required materials: Presenters should prefold the coyote from a large square, and then completely unfold it for storytelling. Paper with contrasting sides creates the best results.

Special notes:
1. Make sure the folded edge is on top in Step #3.
2. Step #5 is a mountain fold. Fold the sides to the back of the model.
3. All the creases must be very firm before attempting to open the figure in the last step. If the model falls apart go back and press the folds again.

The Hand That Feeds Me

Wild animals that live in big cities near **tall buildings...**

(Demonstrate with Step #1.)

...and wild animals that live in small towns near **short buildings...**

(Demonstrate with Step #2.)

...have quickly and easily learned how to cross over **bridges...**

(Demonstrate with Step #3.)

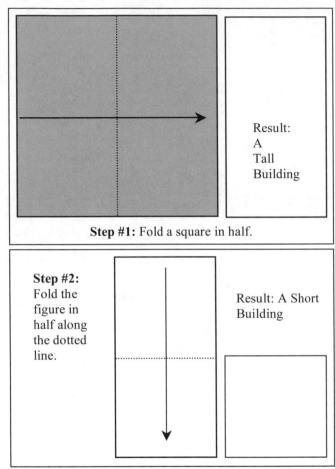

Result:
A
Tall
Building

Step #1: Fold a square in half.

Step #2: Fold the figure in half along the dotted line.

Result: A Short Building

Step #3: Unfold to Step #1. Rotate and position as shown. Fold both sides to the middle, then open slightly so that the figure resembles a bridge with railings.

fold

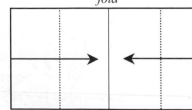

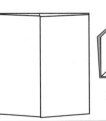

Result: A Bridge

...to visit people's **houses** in search of food, water, and shelter. *(Demonstrate with Step #4.)*

They have adapted to suburban and city habitats and unlike most people, animals don't care one bit if the houses are large or **small.** *(Demonstrate with Step #5.)*

All they're looking for is **one or two corners** *(demonstrate with Step #6)* that contain bird feeders, pet food, or yummy leftovers in garbage cans.

You've probably heard the old saying, 'one person's trash is another person's treasure?' For wild animals, one person's trash is appetizers, dinner, and dessert. Known as opportunistic feeders, many city dwelling animals are true omnivores. They will eat just about anything, including pet cats and dogs.

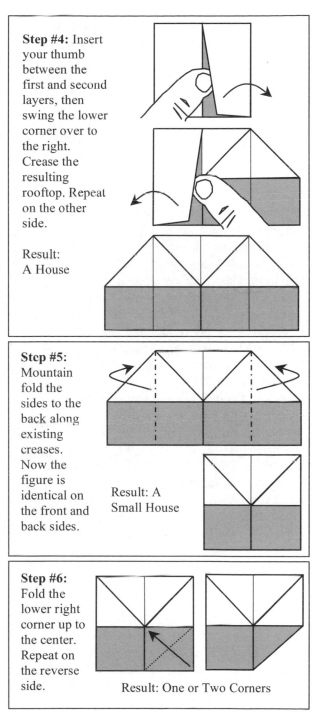

Step #4: Insert your thumb between the first and second layers, then swing the lower corner over to the right. Crease the resulting rooftop. Repeat on the other side.

Result:
A House

Step #5: Mountain fold the sides to the back along existing creases. Now the figure is identical on the front and back sides.

Result: A Small House

Step #6: Fold the lower right corner up to the center. Repeat on the reverse side.

Result: One or Two Corners

35

We may hear them tipping over trashcans or, in the case of skunks, we may smell where they've been, but unless they're trapped and can't escape, we'll probably never see the wild animals that secretly live all around us. For the most part, they **dart** *(demonstrate with Step #7)* about stealthily at night, completely undetected.

The coyote is an especially smart scavenger. He's known as a trickster, so don't be fooled! Most of the time, coyotes go out of their way to avoid people, but in many parks and neighborhoods, they've discovered that we're a good source for food. As they lose their natural habitat and their fear of people, they get bolder and **pop out** of the shadows, putting them and us in danger. *(Demonstrate with Step #8.)*

Should you follow the advice of this trickster? *(Use the origami coyote as a puppet that talks, then bites your hand.)*

"Please don't feed wild animals. Except for me. That's right, mister, you heard me. Feed only me, no other coyotes and especially, don't feed those worthless fleabags, raccoons. And never, ever waste perfectly yummy garbage on bears. That would be a big, smelly mistake, so you'd better check the bottom of your shoes if you let bears eat your trash! Hey lady, why don't you fork over some of those M&M's in your pocket? Don't be afraid. I'd never bite the hand that feeds me, at least, not on purpose…"

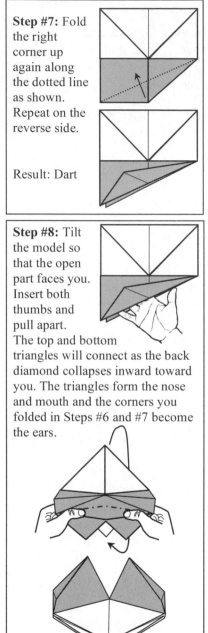

Step #7: Fold the right corner up again along the dotted line as shown. Repeat on the reverse side.

Result: Dart

Step #8: Tilt the model so that the open part faces you. Insert both thumbs and pull apart. The top and bottom triangles will connect as the back diamond collapses inward toward you. The triangles form the nose and mouth and the corners you folded in Steps #6 and #7 become the ears.

Result: The Complete Coyote Puppet

Optional Follow-Up Activities

1. Fold more coyotes with increasingly smaller squares of paper, making sure to label each step with its name from the story. Pairing story events with folding steps greatly enhances short-term memory of both, and using ever smaller paper increases precision.

2. Several fables, legends, and folktales feature coyotes as prominent characters. Identify as many as you can. Do the stories share similar themes or plots? Is the coyote always a trickster? Write your own story about your origami coyote. Make it fanciful, factual, or both!

3. Draw eyes, a nose, and other details on the origami coyote head. Can you figure out how to fold a body, too? Find directions from other origami books, or design your own coyote body by experimenting with some of the folding techniques you've already learned in this book. The first origami paper folders played with paper and kept trying different steps until the paper finally resembled the shape they wanted.

4. Test your knowledge of coyotes by answering true or false to these statements. Answers are on the next page.
   a. Coyote pups enjoy eating their father's vomit.
   b. If coyotes stopped howling, the moon would never be full again.
   c. Coyotes eat berries, rats, and bugs.
   d. The average life expectancy of an adult coyote in the wild is 10 to 15 years.
   e. Like dogs, coyotes are members of the canine family.
   f. Coyotes are sneaky because they're half reptile, half mammal.
   g. Coyotes don't hear well, so they use their nose to sniff out trouble.
   h. Coyotes can jump over an eight-foot fence with a single bound.
   i. Four out of five coyote pups die during their first year of life.
   j. Coyotes eat garbage because they can't run very fast.
   k. Coyotes are modest and only go to the bathroom in one hidden place.
   l. Mountain coyotes have darker fur than desert coyotes.
   m. Coyotes hate dog food, so don't worry about bringing it in the house.

5. Answers to the quiz:
   a. True, that's why garbage tastes so good to them as adults.
   b. False, if they stopped howling, other coyotes would not know where the party is.
   c. True, coyotes are omnivores. They'll eat anything!
   d. True, if coyotes have a steady food supply, they can live as long as similarly sized dogs.
   e. True, coyotes, wolves, jackals, and dogs are all cousins.
   f. False, coyotes are sneaky because they are smart.
   g. False, coyotes have great hearing *and* a great sense of smell.
   h. True, and if they can't jump over a fence, they don't mind digging under it instead.
   i. True, unless the winter is harsh, then even more pups die.
   j. False, coyotes run up to 40 miles per hour. They eat garbage because it tastes better than their father's regurgitated food.
   k. False, coyotes urinate everywhere! That's how they warn other animals to stay away.
   l. True, mountain coyotes are larger, too.
   m. False, dog food is like a gourmet meal to coyotes.

6. Write a play and act out the parts with your origami hand puppets. Make hats for them so they can be costumed like other characters, like park rangers or hikers.

7. Use this story to introduce or complement discussions about:
   a. Problems related to disappearing animal habitats.
   b. Rules for interacting with wild animals.
   c. Canines.
   d. Puppetry.
   e. Native American folklore.

Build this duck in ten easy steps.

About the story: A changing ecosystem creates a haven for migrating birds.

Recommended ages:
Listening only: All ages.
Listening & paper folding: age 6 – adult.

Required materials: Presenters should prefold the duck from a large square, and then completely unfold it for storytelling. Paper with contrasting sides creates the best results.

Special notes:
1. Steps #4 through #7 are only a simple pleat.
2. The entire front of the duck will slide when you lift the head in Step #9. Part of the resulting diagonal valley fold is hidden under the outer layer.
3. *Ducky* means delightful or darling.

A Ducky New Home

Not far from here, a quiet **pond...**

(Hold up a square to represent the pond.)

...is surrounded by **hills...**

(Demonstrate with Step #1.)

...and **young pine trees.**

(Demonstrate with Step #2.)

It's a favorite resting place for migrating ducks and geese, but it wasn't always so well protected. Many years ago, a terrible storm roared through the area and drastically changed the ecosystem.

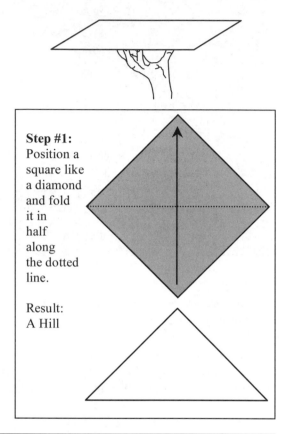

Step #1: Position a square like a diamond and fold it in half along the dotted line.

Result: A Hill

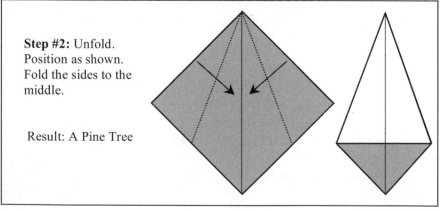

Step #2: Unfold. Position as shown. Fold the sides to the middle.

Result: A Pine Tree

The wind was so strong, several pine trees **broke in half**, like this. *(Demonstrate with Step #3.)*

Eventually some **new growth** sprouted up, *(demonstrate with Step #4)* but then a fire swept up the hill and burned the new growth **down** to the ground. *(Unfold Step #4.)*

More recently, vines have grown **halfway up** the old broken and charred tree trunks. *(Demonstrate with Step #5.)*

The vines twist part way **down**…

(Demonstrate with Step #6.)

…and then twist up again, **almost to the top** of the old dead trees.

(Demonstrate with Step #7.)

New trees are growing, too. They're filling in the hillside quickly since there's been plenty of rain and no more disasters.

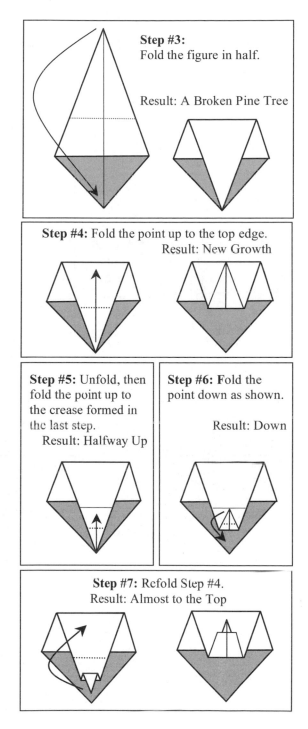

Step #3:
Fold the figure in half.

Result: A Broken Pine Tree

Step #4: Fold the point up to the top edge.
Result: New Growth

Step #5: Unfold, then fold the point up to the crease formed in the last step.
Result: Halfway Up

Step #6: Fold the point down as shown.

Result: Down

Step #7: Refold Step #4.
Result: Almost to the Top

Even though the new trees are only **half** as tall as the ones that were destroyed…

(Demonstrate with Step #8.)

…the quiet pond is home to enough plants, frogs and small fish to **lift…**

(Demonstrate with Step #9.)

…the numbers of birds that drop by during their annual flights through the area in the spring and again in the fall.

Wild ducks often build nests and **raise…**

(Demonstrate with Step #10.)

…families in quiet ponds like this. They don't always migrate, especially if there's enough food and open water all year round.

Who knows? One day this pond might be quacky instead of quiet. Then we'll know that some of our feathered friends have decided to move in and make themselves a ducky new home.

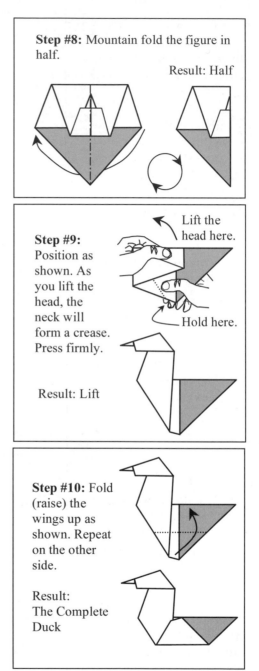

Step #8: Mountain fold the figure in half.

Result: Half

Step #9: Position as shown. As you lift the head, the neck will form a crease. Press firmly.

Lift the head here.

Hold here.

Result: Lift

Step #10: Fold (raise) the wings up as shown. Repeat on the other side.

Result: The Complete Duck

Optional Follow-Up Activities

1. Fold more ducks with increasingly smaller squares of paper, making sure to label each step with its name from the story. Pairing story events with folding steps greatly enhances short-term memory of both, and using ever smaller paper increases precision.

2. Experiment with variously textured papers or starched fabric, including wallpaper, freezer wrap, construction paper, wrapping paper, foil, cotton, and linen.

3. Use the origami ducks as nametags, bulletin board decorations, ornaments, place marks, or lace with yarn for necklaces. Glue tiny ducks to earring posts or string several together like beaded jewelry.

4. Research the actual colors and markings of different species of ducks, and then draw these characteristics on the origami model. Attach a short summary about the featured duck. Include its scientific name and facts about its habitat, diet, and size.

5. Test your knowledge of ducks by answering true or false to these statements. Answers are on the next page.
   a. Ducks chew their food with 16 teeth.
   b. Newly hatched ducks can float because they're so cute and fat.
   c. Ducks eat plants, fish, and stale bread.
   d. The average life expectancy of a wild duck is 2 to 12 years.
   e. Ducks began growing webbed feet after the intro-*duck*-tion of the Internet.
   f. A duckling learns to recognize its mother while still in the egg.
   g. Duck eggs usually take 28 days to hatch.
   h. Ducks raised on farms could find food in the wild if they had to.
   i. Ducks waddle to show off their tail feathers.
   j. Ducks can swim underwater.
   k. People stuff duck feathers into pillows so their guests will sneeze all night and go home sooner.
   l. Flyways are nesting areas near airports.
   m. Male ducks are brightly colored, while the females have brown or gray feathers
   n. Duck feet are never cold, even in icy cold water.
   o. Like some types of bad mail, a duck's mouth is called a bill.

6. Answers to the quiz:
   a. False, ducks are birds and birds don't have teeth.
   b. False, ducklings are cute, but it's their buoyant feathers that keep them floating, not their chubbiness.
   c. True, many ducks are omnivores, but too much bread isn't good for them.
   d. True, depending on food supply and hunting regulations.
   e. False, ducks always had webbed feet for swimming, not surfing the World Wide Web, although this is a very funny question.
   f. True, mother ducks exchange low calls with their babies before hatching.
   g. True, or a month (in February).
   h. False, wild ducks learn how to forage from their parents. Farm ducks starve in the wild.
   i. False, let's see you walk straight with webbed feet!
   j. True, but not all ducks can dive.
   k. False, duck feathers are soft, warm, and cozy.
   l. False, flyways are known routes for migrating birds.
   m. True, female ducks place a higher value on inner beauty.
   n. False, duck feet are cold, but ducks can't *feel* the cold because their feet have no nerves or blood vessels.
   o. True, but ducks' bills are less expensive.

7. Use this story to introduce or complement discussions about:
   a. The effect of storms or fire on an ecosystem.
   b. Pond plants and animals.
   c. Birds.
   d. Reforestation.
   e. Migration. How do ducks fly such great distances without getting lost?

This traditional butterfly is lovely to look at and easy to make.

About the story: The characteristics and habitat of the Rocky Mountain Bee Plant is described and illustrated by origami folds.

Recommended ages:
Listening only: All ages.
Listening & paper folding: age 7 – adult.

Required materials: Presenters should prefold the butterfly from a large square, and then completely unfold it for storytelling.

Special notes:
1. Step #6 looks at the underside of the figure. Return it to its regular flat position for the next folding step.
2. Press very firmly through all eight layers in Step #7.
3. Pinch the top of the butterfly wings to refine its shape.

Wildflower Power

The Great Plains cover a large part of the central **half** of North America. *(Demonstrate with Step #1.)*

This vast **area of prairie** land stretches 500 miles from east to west and 2000 miles from north to south. *(Demonstrate with Step #2. Point to the narrow width as you say 500 miles. Point to the length of the figure as you say 2000 miles.)*

Part of the eastern edge of the Great Plains is formed by the **Red River of the North.** It flows northward into Manitoba along the eastern borders of North and South Dakota. *(Demonstrate with Step #3.)* The rest of the eastern edge runs southward all the way to central Texas.

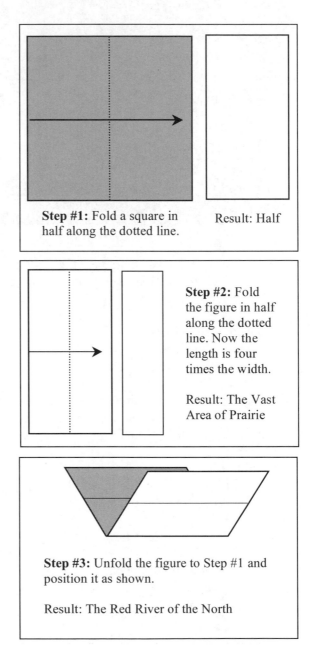

Step #1: Fold a square in half along the dotted line.

Result: Half

Step #2: Fold the figure in half along the dotted line. Now the length is four times the width.

Result: The Vast Area of Prairie

Step #3: Unfold the figure to Step #1 and position it as shown.

Result: The Red River of the North

Most of the western edge of the Great Plains is formed by the **Rocky Mountains.** *(Demonstrate with Step #4.)*

Throughout all this wide expanse of land there are many **pockets** *(demonstrate with Step #5)* where wildflowers flourish.

One of the most common wildflowers is the Rocky Mountain Bee Plant. It has several pink or purple clusters of small flowers that each have **four long petals** that look like this. *(Demonstrate with Step #6. Separate the folds, hold on top, and tilt the figure to expose the four flower petals underneath.)*

Six long parts called stamens surround the petals. The stamens look so much like spider legs that some people call it the spiderflower.

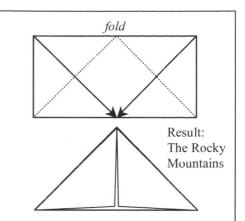

fold

Result: The Rocky Mountains

Step #4: Position the figure with the fold on top. Fold both corners down as shown.

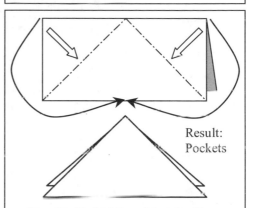

Result: Pockets

Step #5: Unfold Step #4 and collapse both corners into the figure as shown. This is known as the bird bomb base.

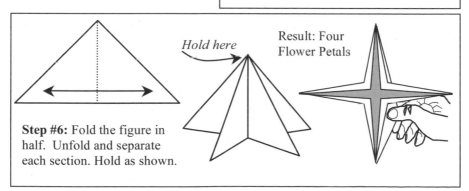

Hold here

Result: Four Flower Petals

Step #6: Fold the figure in half. Unfold and separate each section. Hold as shown.

The Rocky Mountain Bee Plant grows on flat-topped areas called **mesas**, too. *(Demonstrate with Step #7.)*

As it **grows taller**, *(demonstrate with Step #8)* the scent of the flower naturally gets stronger.

Some people **cover** their noses *(demonstrate with Step #9)* and call it Stinkweed.

Obviously, based on the name of the flower, bees are **open** *(demonstrate with Step #10)* to the smell of the Rocky Mountain Bee Plant. But they aren't the only ones. Butterflies like it, too.

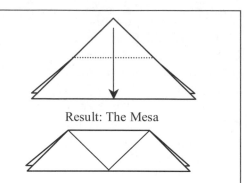

Result: The Mesa

Step #7: Fold the top point of the pyramid down to the bottom edge. Press firmly through all layers.

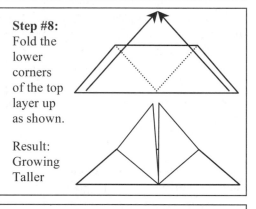

Step #8: Fold the lower corners of the top layer up as shown.

Result: Growing Taller

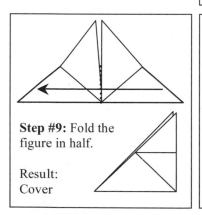

Step #9: Fold the figure in half.

Result: Cover

Step #10: Hold the lower edge as shown and **open** both wings. Press only half way up the butterfly.

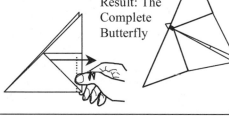

Result: The Complete Butterfly

Optional Follow-Up Activities

1. Fold more butterflies with increasingly smaller squares of paper, making sure to label each step with its name from the story. Pairing story events with folding steps greatly enhances short-term memory of both, and using ever smaller paper increases precision.

2. Experiment with variously textured papers and starched fabrics, including wallpaper, freezer wrap, construction paper, wrapping paper, foil, cotton, and linen.

3. Butterflies represent many different things to people worldwide. Research butterfly mythology. Make a different origami butterfly and label it for each symbol you find. For example, butterflies represent young girls in Japan.

4. Research the actual colors and markings of different species of butterflies, and then draw these characteristics on the origami model. Attach a short summary about the featured butterfly. Include its scientific name and facts about its habitat, diet, and size.

5. Test your knowledge of butterflies by answering true or false to these statements. Answers are on the next page.
   a. Butterflies range in size from 1/8 inch to almost 12 inches.
   b. Butterflies hear very well.
   c. Butterflies eat berries, seeds, and other insects.
   d. The average life expectancy of a butterfly is 14 - 30 days.
   e. Butterflies emerge from cocoons.
   f. Butterflies migrate thousands of miles.
   g. Butterflies are considered a harmful pest to farmers.
   h. Both butterflies and moths belong to the order Lepidoptera.
   i. Butterflies use their antennae to pick up radio stations.
   j. Some butterflies only have four legs.
   k. Butterfly wings are covered with scales.
   l. Only queen butterflies lay eggs.
   m. Like people, male butterflies are usually bigger than females.
   n. Butterflies taste with their feet.

6. Answers to the quiz:
   a. True, most butterflies are two to four inches from wing to wing.
   b. False, butterflies only feel vibrations. They do not hear sounds.
   c. False, butterflies don't have mouths. Instead, they have a straw-like proboscis that's used to drink fluids from plants.
   d. True, although the Brimstone butterfly can live up to ten months.
   e. False, moths spin soft cocoons. Butterflies develop inside hard-shelled chrysalis.
   f. True, Monarch butterflies journey from the Great Lakes to the Gulf of Mexico, over 2,000 miles.
   g. False, butterflies are helpful pollinators.
   h. True, in Greek, Lepidoptera means *scale wing.*
   i. False, butterflies can't hear music and dislike talk radio.
   j. False, all butterflies are insects and have six legs. Sometimes the front two legs are hard to see because they are tucked in close to the butterfly's body.
   k. True, the wings are translucent. The scales give them color and patterns.
   l. False, there's no royalty among butterflies. All females lay eggs.
   m. False, female butterflies are larger than males.
   n. True, they don't wear smelly shoes, so flowers taste good.

7. Find and build other origami butterflies. Organize the instructions according to the number of folding steps or level of difficulty.

8. Use this story to introduce or complement discussions about:
   a. Wildflowers and their habitats and characteristics.
   b. Insects. How are butterflies and bees alike and different?
   c. Greek roots of scientific words (Lepidoptera, chrysalis).
   d. Ecosystem of prairies.
   e. North American geography and the Great Plains.
   f. Plants and plant parts.

Create this elegant Trillium blossom in nine easy steps.

About the story: Myrmecochory is a botanical term for "seed dispersal by ants." The process is described and illustrated by nine progressive origami folds.

Recommended ages:
Listening only: All ages.
Listening & paper folding: age 7 – adult.

Required materials: Presenters should prefold the flower from a large square, and then completely unfold it for storytelling. Trillium blossoms are often white, so using green and white paper with contrasting sides creates the most realistic results.

Special notes:
1. Make sure the taller protruding point in Step #5 ends up between the second and third layers.
2. Step #8 locks the figure and prevents the flower from separating.
3. The flower can be shaped according to individual preferences in Step #9. Trillium petals are round and wide.

Hidden Farms Beneath Our Feet

*Myrmecology is the scientific study of ants. During the last two hundred years, myrmecologists have found ants all over the world. *(Demonstrate by holding up a whole square to represent the whole world.)*

There are only two places where ants do not live, the **North and South Poles.** *(Demonstrate with Step #1. Point to the top as the North Pole and the bottom as the South Pole.)*

There are more ants than any other type of animal. Did you know that ants have six legs, two eyes, the largest of all insect brains, and two stomachs? **One stomach** stores food for the ant itself and the **second stomach** stores food for the ant's friends and neighbors. *(Demonstrate with Step #2. Each corner represents a stomach.)*

*mur-mah-COL-ah-gee

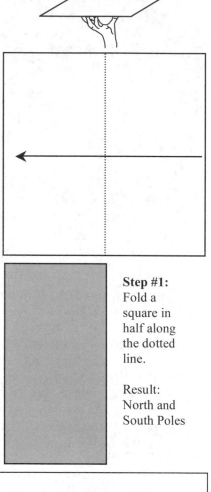

Step #1: Fold a square in half along the dotted line.

Result: North and South Poles

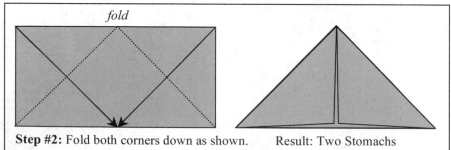

fold

Step #2: Fold both corners down as shown.   Result: Two Stomachs

Ants live in huge numbers in highly organized and very tidy colonies deep in **the ground** or deep **inside** trees or logs. *(Demonstrate with Step #3. The first corner is the ground. The second corner is a log.)*

The head of the ant has a pair of large, strong **jaws** that can lift 20 times its own body weight. The jaws open and shut sideways like a pair of scissors. *(Demonstrate with Step #4.)*

They also have antennae on top of their heads, which they use for touching and smelling. *(Demonstrate with Step #5.)*

If an ant finds food, it leaves a trail of scent so that the other ants in the colony can find it. Each ant colony has its own unique smell so intruders are sniffed out immediately.

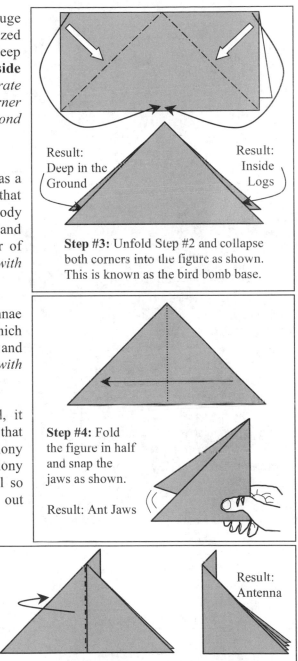

Result: Deep in the Ground

Result: Inside Logs

Step #3: Unfold Step #2 and collapse both corners into the figure as shown. This is known as the bird bomb base.

Step #4: Fold the figure in half and snap the jaws as shown.

Result: Ant Jaws

Result: Antenna

Step #5: Valley fold the first two layers to the right. Mountain fold the 3rd and 4th layers to the right. The tall middle section is between the 2nd and 3rd layers.

Some ants are ranchers that take care of herds of aphids. Aphids are tiny insects that make a liquid called honeydew. The ants eat the honeydew and in turn provide food for the aphids.

Other ants are farmers that **raise** crops. *(Demonstrate with Step #6.)*

The ants **gather up** specific edible seeds, *(demonstrate with Step #7)*

...take them underground to their nest, eat just the tasty outer part, and put the rest of the seed **into** their garbage. *(Demonstrate with Step #8.)*

The ant trash becomes a fertile and protected farm for the plant. The next year, a new plant grows, produces more seeds for the ants to eat, and the farming operation continues, year after year.

Trillium is one of many plants whose seeds are spread by ants. *(Demonstrate with Step #9.)* It grows in shaded woodlands throughout most of North America. Trillium has three large petals and is one of the first flowers to bloom in the spring. But it wouldn't bloom at all if it weren't for the hidden farms beneath our feet.

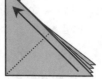
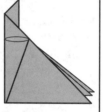

Step #6: Fold only the top layer up as shown.   Result: Raise

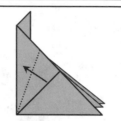

Step #7: Fold the same layer up to the middle again.   Result: Gather Up

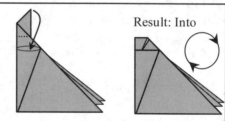

Result: Into

Step #8: Fold the point down and tuck it into the pocket formed in the last step.

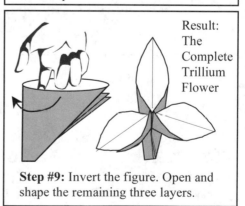

Result: The Complete Trillium Flower

Step #9: Invert the figure. Open and shape the remaining three layers.

Optional Follow-Up Activities

1. Fold more flowers with increasingly smaller squares of paper, making sure to label each step with its name from the story. Pairing story events with folding steps greatly enhances short-term memory of both, and using ever smaller paper increases precision.

2. Experiment with variously textured papers, including wallpaper, freezer wrap, construction paper, wrapping paper, and foil

3. This design can be folded successfully out of starched fabric. For best results, use a non-fraying fabric or hem the raw edges before folding. Finish with a hot iron to make the creases permanent.

4. Research the actual colors and markings of different species of trillium, and then draw these characteristics on the origami model. Attach a short summary about the featured plant. Include its scientific name and facts about its habitat.

5. Test your knowledge of ants by answering true or false to these statements. Answers are on the next page.
   a. Ants have the smallest insect brain.
   b. Ants can be green, red, brown, yellow, blue or purple in color.
   c. The combined weight of the world's ants is greater than the combined weight of the world's humans.
   d. The average life expectancy of an ant is 45-60 days.
   e. Adult ants cannot chew or swallow solid food.
   f. Like people, ants have just one stomach.
   g. Ants can lift 200 times their own body weight.
   h. Antarctica got its name because ants live there.
   i. Ants use their antennae only for touch.
   j. Really fast ants have eight legs.
   k. Ant bodies are covered with a hard armor called an exoskeleton.
   l. Only Queen ants lay eggs.
   m. Queen ants get their name because their heads are shaped like crowns.
   n. Ants are solitary, uncooperative, untidy insects that prefer to live alone.

6. Answers to the quiz:
    a. False, ants have the largest insect brain.
    b. True, ants can be many colors.
    c. True, there are SO MANY ants in the world!
    d. True, but wood ants can live up to 10 years.
    e. True, ants can only eat the juice they squeeze out of seeds, insects, and other yummy foods.
    f. False, ants have two stomachs.
    g. False, ants can only lift 20 times their own body weight.
    h. False, there are no ants at the South Pole.
    i. False, ants use their antennae for touch *and* smelling.
    j. False, all ants have six legs.
    k. True, ants are insects. All insects have exoskeletons.
    l. True, only queen ants lay eggs. Every colony must have at least one queen in order to survive.
    m. False, ants have smooth round heads.
    n. False, false, false in every way.

7. Find and build other origami flower designs. Make a bouquet or centerpiece for a special occasion. Organize the instructions according to the number of folding steps or level of difficulty.

8. Myrmecochory is a botanical term for "seed dispersal by ants." Find out what other plants besides trillium are helped by ants. Make a poster displaying your results. Include drawings, photographs, and maps.

9. Use this story to introduce or complement discussions about:
    a. Wildflowers and their habitats and characteristics.
    b. Insects.
    c. Greek roots of scientific words.
    d. Ants.
    e. Farming, ranching, or gardening.

This traditional rabbit is constructed in seven easy steps.

About the story: Learning to be patient and pay attention yields rewards at the park.

Recommended ages:
   Listening only: All ages.
   Listening & paper folding: age 7 – adult.

Required materials: Presenters should prefold the rabbit from a large square, and then completely unfold it for storytelling.

Special notes:
1. The creases made in the preliminary folds help Step #3 fall into place.
2. Point to the lower corners to emphasize the butterfly wings in Step #5.
3. Cover the lower points (which become bunny ears) in Steps #7 and #8 to draw attention to the upper part of the figure.

A Bench on a Bridge

Preliminary Folds:
Fold a square as shown, and then completely unfold it before you begin.

Resulting Creases

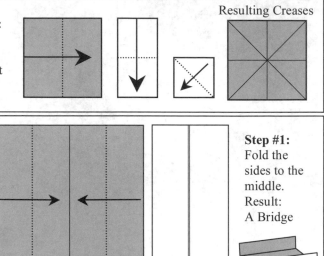

A rickety old wood **foot-bridge** crosses a creek on a hiking trail in a park not far from here. *(Demonstrate with Step #1.)*

Step #1:
Fold the sides to the middle.
Result:
A Bridge

It has a **high-backed bench** attached to one of its railings. *(Demonstrate with Step #2.)*

Step #2:
Fold the bottom edge up to the midline.

Result: A Bench

The bench is shaded by a grove of ancient **trees** that have the longest branches and the widest trunks in the whole park. *(Demonstrate with Step #3.)*

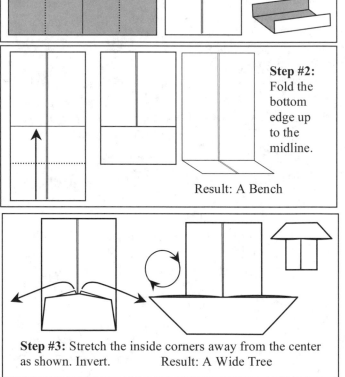

Step #3: Stretch the inside corners away from the center as shown. Invert.   Result: A Wide Tree

I sit on the high-backed bench every time I walk on the trail. The last time I was there, the weather was hot and the air felt heavy, like an old musty curtain in a run-down theatre. I was alone. The forest was completely still and silent until suddenly, a **woodpecker** began hammering against one of the trees. *(Demonstrate with Step #4.)*

I tried to find it in the thick branches, but it stopped hammering and I didn't know where to look anymore. That's when I noticed that the forest was not nearly as still or as quiet as I thought it was.

A leaf drifted down and landed near my foot. A twig snapped somewhere on the other side of the bridge. A crow squawked overhead. And as I paid closer attention to the subtle movements and sounds around me, a **butterfly** landed on a tiny purple flower that I hadn't even noticed before. *(Demonstrate with Step #5.)*

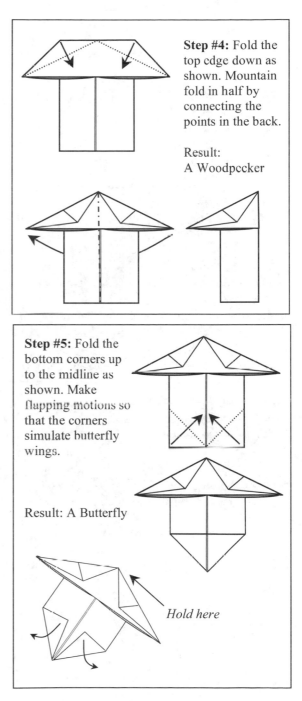

Step #4: Fold the top edge down as shown. Mountain fold in half by connecting the points in the back.

Result:
A Woodpecker

Step #5: Fold the bottom corners up to the midline as shown. Make flapping motions so that the corners simulate butterfly wings.

Result: A Butterfly

Hold here

The ground was muddy and marked with several **three-toed tracks.** *(Demonstrate with Step #6.)* A bird that flew away when I first stepped onto the bridge must have left them behind. *(Demonstrate with Step #7.)*

I wondered what kind of bird it was and whether or not it would return if I was really, really quiet. I waited and waited, and just as I was about to give up, the purple flower trembled and a little pink **bunny** nose popped out. *(Press both legs down and rotate the model as shown.)*

The rabbit stared at me for a few seconds and then it hopped lazily under the bridge. I heard a few more creatures snapping twigs and calling out to each other, but I only saw two all day, the rabbit and the butterfly. I wonder how many saw me?

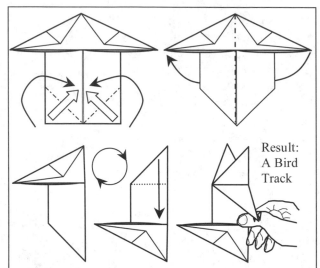

Result: A Bird Track

Step #6: Unfold the lower corners and collapse them into the figure. Mountain fold the whole figure in half as before. Rotate the figure and position as shown. Let the outer layers spread open on both sides. Hold as shown and tilt the figure to emphasize the top points. They represent the 3-toed bird tracks.

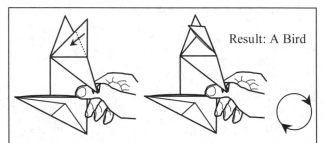

Result: A Bird

Step #7: Fold the point. Hold as shown and make flapping motions to simulate a bird. Press the legs forward and rotate to complete the rabbit.

The Complete Rabbit

Optional Follow-Up Activities

1. Fold more rabbits with increasingly smaller squares of paper, making sure to label each step with its name from the story. Pairing story events with folding steps greatly enhances short-term memory of both, and using ever smaller paper increases precision.

2. Experiment with variously textured papers, including wallpaper, freezer wrap, construction paper, wrapping paper, and foil.

3. Read two other Storigami rabbit stories: "The Rabbits of Rainbow Mountain" in *Holiday Folding Stories* and "After School Adventure" in *Folding Stories,* both written by Christine Petrell Kallevig.

4. This story is set in a park "not far from here." Do you know where it is? Have you sat on that same bench? Write a story about what you heard, felt, and saw while you were at the park. Use other origami animals from this book to illustrate your story.

5. Test your knowledge of rabbits by answering true or false to these statements. Answers are on the next page.
   a. Rabbit teeth never stop growing.
   b. Rabbits and deer share the same names for their males (bucks) and females (does).
   c. Groups of baby rabbits are called litters of kits.
   d. Rabbits can whistle.
   e. Adult rabbits have 200 teeth.
   f. Warren is a city for people, not rabbits.
   g. Unlike people who eat too much candy, rabbits cannot vomit.
   h. Newborn rabbits have a sweet smell.
   i. Rabbits use their nose only for trying to look cute while posing for photographers.
   j. Giant rabbits were used like horses by early American cowboys.
   k. Rabbits hibernate all winter.
   l. Rabbits lay colorful eggs in the spring.
   m. Rabbits sweat through the pads of their feet.
   n. Rabbits are so friendly and peaceful they never bite people.

6. Answers to the quiz:
    a. True, that's why rabbits like to chew so much.
    b. True, and a group of rabbits is called a herd, too.
    c. True, this is similar to litters of kittens.
    d. True, but rabbits whistle only when very distressed.
    e. False, rabbits only have 28 teeth.
    f. False, more than 50 locations are named Warren, but a rabbit home is called a warren, too.
    g. True, rabbits don't throw up.
    h. False, newborn rabbits have no smell at all.
    i. False, rabbits use their nose for smelling and looking cute.
    j. False, this is a tall tale.
    k. False, rabbits do not hibernate. Some turn white in winter, though.
    l. False, hens lay the eggs and rabbits deliver them.
    m. True, it's too embarrassing to sweat anywhere else.
    n. False. Need proof? Hold one by its ears.

7. Find and build other origami rabbits. Make a warren. Organize the instructions according to the number of folding steps or level of difficulty.

8. Use this story to introduce or complement discussions about:
    a. Lagomorphs and their habitats and characteristics.
    b. Woodpeckers and other woodland birds.
    c. Animal tracks that have three toes.
    d. Hiking etiquette and safety procedures.
    e. Learning to focus and pay attention.

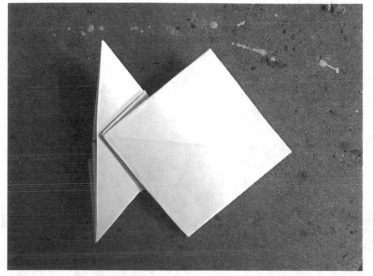

This sturdy fish is folded in eight easy steps.

About the story: Common characteristics of fish are described and illustrated by origami folds.

Recommended ages:
Listening only: All ages.
Listening & paper folding: age 7 – adult.

Required materials: Presenters should prefold a fish from a large square, and then completely unfold it for storytelling.

Special notes:
1. Make sure you turn the figure over to the reverse side between Step #6 and #7.
2. After "gliding" the figure in Step #7, restore it to its point-facing-up position before its final fold.
3. Press the final figure firmly through all layers to keep its shape intact.

Hey, There's Something Fishy Going On

An *ichthyologist is a person who studies fish. Ichthyologists have identified almost 25,000 different species of fish, more than all the species of amphibians, reptiles, birds and mammals combined.

Fish live all over the **world** *(hold up a square to represent the world).* They are vertebrate animals, which means they all have a **backbone.** *(Demonstrate with Step #1.)*

Fish come in many sizes, shapes, and colors, but all fish have **fins**, live in water, and most breathe with gills. *(Demonstrate with Step #2.)*

*ick-thee-ALL-oh-jist

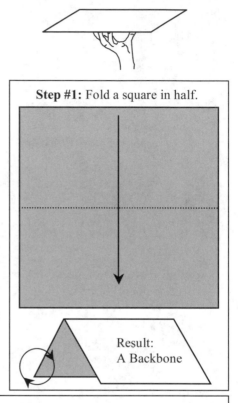

Step #1: Fold a square in half.

Result: A Backbone

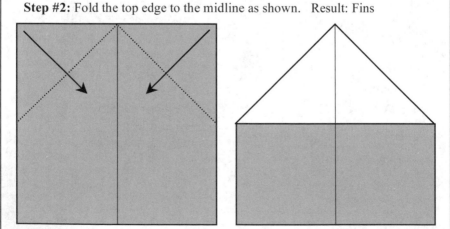

Step #2: Fold the top edge to the midline as shown.   Result: Fins

64

Most fish see quite well, but they also have a specialized sense organ called the lateral line. *(Point to the midline of the figure.)*

It works like radar and helps them navigate in dark or murky water.

Fish are cold-blooded, which means their **inside** *(demonstrate with Step #3)* body temperature is the same as the temperature of the surrounding water.

If the water temperature gets **lower** *(demonstrate with Step #4)* their body temperature gets lower, too.

There are more bony fish than any other type. They have jaws, bony skeletons, hard **scales** on the outside *(demonstrate with Step #5)* and a **swim bladder** on the inside. *(Demonstrate with Step #6.)* It fills with air and helps fish balance while swimming or floating in place.

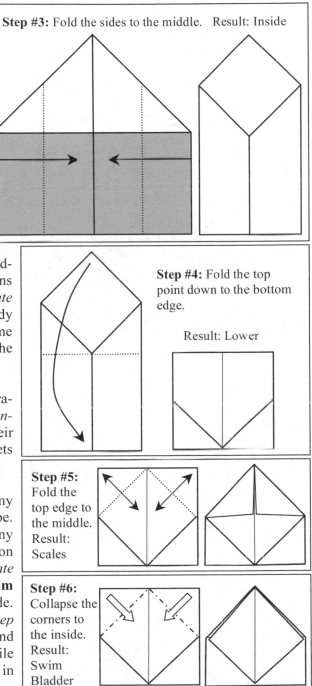

Step #3: Fold the sides to the middle.   Result: Inside

Step #4: Fold the top point down to the bottom edge.

Result: Lower

Step #5: Fold the top edge to the middle. Result: Scales

Step #6: Collapse the corners to the inside. Result: Swim Bladder

65

Fish that we keep as pets in our **houses** *(turn the model over)* are almost always bony fish.

Sharks and rays are a different type of fish. They have skeletons made of cartilage instead of bone. Sharks and rays have gills and scales like bony fish, but no swim bladders. If they ever stop **gliding** through the water, they'll sink like a rock to the bottom of the ocean. *(Demonstrate with Step #7.)*

Fish grown in unpolluted water are a good source of nutrition for our brains, but research studies have found that kids who keep live fish as pets benefit in other ways, too. They earn higher **grades** and they get higher **test scores**, too. *(Demonstrate with Step #8. The first corner is grades. The second corner is test scores.)*

Who knew taking care of fish makes you smarter? Maybe that happens because fish are more educated than other animals, you know, because they swim in schools? (Ha ha, very *finny…*)

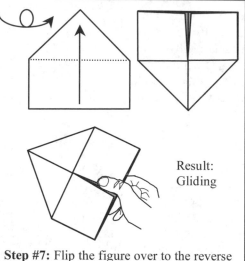

Result: Gliding

Step #7: Flip the figure over to the reverse side for the house, then fold the bottom edge up to the top. Hold as shown. Make gliding motions, like a ray swimming in the water.

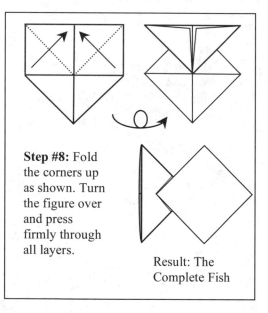

Step #8: Fold the corners up as shown. Turn the figure over and press firmly through all layers.

Result: The Complete Fish

Optional Follow-Up Activities

1. Fold more fish with increasingly smaller squares of paper, making sure to label each step with its name from the story. Pairing story events with folding steps greatly enhances short-term memory of both, and using ever smaller paper increases precision.

2. Find and build other origami fish. Organize the instructions according to the number of folding steps or level of difficulty.

3. Fish are important characters in many worldwide legends, folktales, and myths. Make a list of as many as you can find. Are fish weak or powerful in these stories? Write your own story or poem about fish. Include other animals you learned to fold in this book.

4. Research the actual colors and markings of different species of fish, and then draw these characteristics on the origami model. Attach a short summary about the featured fish. Include its scientific name and facts about its habitat, diet, and size.

5. Test your knowledge of fish by answering true or false to these statements. Answers are on the next page.
   a. There are three distinct groups of fish.
   b. "Slippery as an eel" is not an exaggeration.
   c. Fish stink.
   d. The largest fish is a blue whale.
   e. Fish have teeth but can't chew.
   f. Fish have eyelids so water won't get in their eyes.
   g. Tunas can swim up to 50 miles an hour.
   h. Dogfish got their name because they chase catfish.
   i. A freshly hatched fish is called a fry.
   j. All fish must stay underwater or they'll die.
   k. Pet goldfish have survived for more than 40 years.
   l. Fish group together in schools to make themselves look larger.
   m. The world's smallest fish is less than one half inch long, fully grown.
   n. Fish are actually brown. They only look colorful because of an optical illusion through the water.

6. Answers to the quiz:
    a. True, the three groups of fish are bony, cartilaginous, and jawless.
    b. True, eels are a type of jawless fish that secrete protective mucus on their skin.
    c. True, but only if they have been allowed to spoil. Fresh fish are odorless.
    d. False, whales aren't fish, they're mammals. The largest fish is a whale shark.
    e. True, chewing interferes with the passage of water over the gills so fish would suffocate if they chewed their food.
    f. False, most fish don't have eyelids, but sharks do.
    g. True, but only for short distances. A steady speed for strong swimmers is five to ten miles per hour.
    h. False, dogfish are sharks and live in the ocean. Most catfish live in freshwater, so dogfish don't bother them at all.
    i. True, not broil, not bake, and especially not barbeque.
    j. False, fish can be out of water for a short time without harm.
    k. True, the oldest goldfish was 45 when it finally went belly up.
    l. True, smaller fish are more vulnerable to predators so there's safety in groups.
    m. True, the smallest fish is the Philippine goby.
    n. False, some fish are brown, but they're all other colors, too.

7. Use this story to introduce or complement discussions about:
    a. Water pollution and its effect on fish.
    b. Fish as pets.
    c. Greek roots in scientific words.
    d. Fossilized fish finds. How old are fish?
    e. Overfishing. Will fish of the future live in tanks?

Hop along happily with this friendly little toad.

About the story: The metamorphosis of toads, from tadpole to adult, is described and illustrated with origami.

Recommended ages:
Listening only: All ages.
Listening & paper folding: age 8 – adult.

Required materials: The 8.5 in. x 2.5 in. strip remaining after cutting letter-sized paper into a square is perfect for this toad. Presenters should prefold a toad from double or triple sized paper, and then completely unfold it for storytelling.

Special notes:
1. Illustrations for Steps #3 - #5 show only the top portion of the figure.
2. Step #7 extends the whole length of the model, including under the triangle at the top of the figure.
3. Make the toad jump by pressing down, then slipping off the pleated leg. Use your fingernail for best results.

Toadly Awesome

The name amphibian means double life *(demonstrate with Step #1)* and is given to animals that live partly in water and partly on land. (*One side is water, the other side is land.*)

Amphibians are found everywhere except Antarctica and the Arctic Circle. There are three basic types: frogs and toads, salamanders, and legless wormlike creatures called caecilians (seh SILL yuns) that live in the wetlands of hot jungles. *(Demonstrate with Step #2, and then unfold everything.)*

Both toads and frogs develop from fishlike tadpoles that hatch from gooey eggs deposited in shallow water by mothers they will never meet. Tadpoles are dark brown or black and hide in muddy wetland bottoms. They eat algae and decayed plants; have long tails, no legs, and gills on both sides of their heads. *(Demonstrate with Step #3. Lift the corners to simulate gills breathing in and out.)*

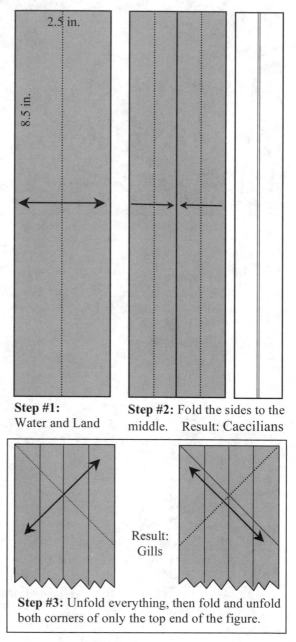

Step #1: Water and Land

Step #2: Fold the sides to the middle. Result: Caecilians

Result: Gills

Step #3: Unfold everything, then fold and unfold both corners of only the top end of the figure.

All amphibians are vertebrates, which means they have a **backbone.** *(Demonstrate with Step #4.)*

Most frog and toad eggs never hatch, and of those that do, turtles, fish, and birds eat most of the resulting tadpoles. Nature is cruel at times, but it has a way of maintaining a proper balance between animals and the environment. That's why the entire planet isn't "toadly" *(totally)* hopping with too many amphibians.

Surviving tadpoles undergo a six to ten week process called metamorphosis as they change into adults that can leave the water and live on land.

Breathing regular atmospheric air is necessary on land, so both of the tadpole gills transform into **lungs.** *(Demonstrate with Step #5.)*

Eventually four legs sprout, the skin color and texture changes, and finally, the tadpole **tail** disappears. *(Demonstrate with Step #6.)*

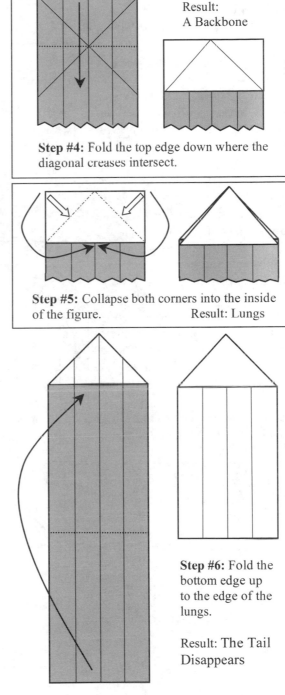

Result:
A Backbone

Step #4: Fold the top edge down where the diagonal creases intersect.

Step #5: Collapse both corners into the inside of the figure.   Result: Lungs

Step #6: Fold the bottom edge up to the edge of the lungs.

Result: The Tail Disappears

When new frogs and toads pop **up** from underwater *(demonstrate with Step #7)* they stop eating plants and begin eating insects by the thousands! Frogs are more vulnerable to predators than toads because toads secrete a bad smelling substance that's poisonous to many animals.

Young frogs and toads are about **half** the length they were as tadpoles but they **grow longer** and the outer layer of their skin **thickens** as they continue to age. *(Demonstrate with the three parts of Step #8.)*

Toads are nocturnal. They venture far away from their birth water at night and hide under **logs and shrubs...** *(Demonstrate with Step #9)*

...at **sunrise** each morning. *(Demonstrate with Step #10.)*

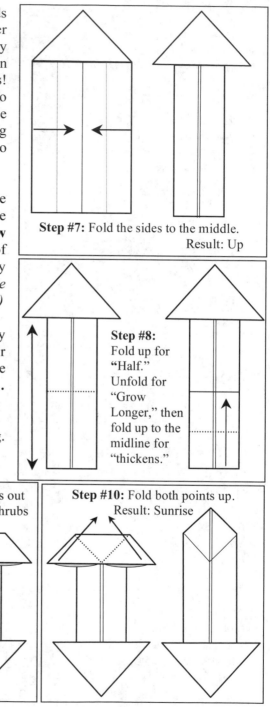

Step #7: Fold the sides to the middle.
Result: Up

Step #8:
Fold up for "Half."
Unfold for "Grow Longer," then fold up to the midline for "thickens."

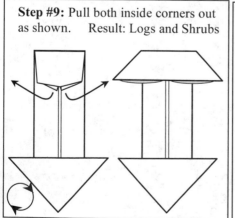

Step #9: Pull both inside corners out as shown.   Result: Logs and Shrubs

Step #10: Fold both points up.
Result: Sunrise

Frogs stay close to wetlands because unlike the dry and warty texture of toads, frog skin is smooth and requires constant moisture. Both frogs and toads can absorb water and oxygen through their skin, which allows them to stay underwater for a long time with just their **eyes** showing above the surface. *(Demonstrate with Step #11.)*

The **front legs** of both frogs and toads are short and stubby. *(Demonstrate with Step #12.)*

One of the main differences between them is their back legs. The back legs of toads are about **half** as long as the back legs of frogs. *(Demonstrate with Step #13.)*

Longer back legs enable frogs to leap, but toads can only jump or crawl. *(Demonstrate with Step #14.)*

I wonder which amphibian we made today, a frog or a toad?

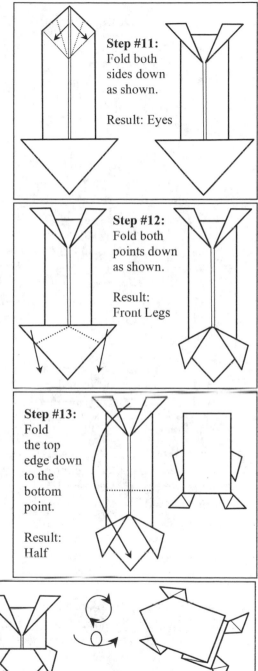

Step #11:
Fold both sides down as shown.

Result: Eyes

Step #12:
Fold both points down as shown.

Result: Front Legs

Step #13:
Fold the top edge down to the bottom point.

Result: Half

Step #14: Fold the same edge back up to create a pleated, springy leg.

Result: The Complete Toad

73

Optional Follow-Up Activities

1. Fold more toads with increasingly smaller strips of paper, making sure to label each step with its name from the story. Pairing story events with folding steps greatly enhances short-term memory of both, and using ever smaller paper increases precision.

2. Try folding the toad from a dollar bill.

3. Organize a long jump contest. Draw a starting point in the center of a piece of paper. Place the toad nose on that point and make the toad jump. Mark where the toad nose lands. Give each "toadtestant" three jumps. Color code the results for each jumper, or let everyone have his own long jump pit. Measure and record the distance between the starting and ending points and chart the results. Make miniature medals for winners. Compare and contrast the jumping results of toads made from differently textured or sized papers. Does heavier, thicker paper result in longer jumps? Do miniature toads jump further? What makes the winning toad the best jumper? Is it folded more precisely, or is the jumping technique better?

4. Research the actual colors and markings of different species of toads and frogs, and then draw these characteristics on the origami model. Attach a short summary about the featured animal. Include its scientific name and facts about its habitat, diet, and size.

5. Several fables, legends, and folktales feature toads and frogs as prominent characters. Identify as many as you can. Do the stories share similar themes or plots? Write your own story about your origami toad. Make it fanciful, factual, or both!

6. Find and build other origami frog designs. Make a display showing the various styles and instructions. Compare numbers of folding steps and levels of difficulty.

7. Use this story to introduce or complement discussions about:
    a. Habitats and characteristics of amphibians.
    b. Frog deformities. Are they linked to pollution?
    c. The ecology of wetlands.
    d. Mythology associated with toads. Do they cause warts?
    e. Does climate change effect amphibians?

For More Information...

National Organizations: The following non-profit organizations provide newsletters, web sites, and listings for regional groups. They also sponsor special events and distribute books and supplies. Membership is easily obtained online by entering them in Internet search engines or by inquiring at the addresses listed below:

International Storytelling Center
116 W. Main St.
Jonesborough, TN 37659
www.storytellingfoundation.net

Origami USA
15 West 77 Street
New York, NY 10024
www.origami-usa.org

Books that combine stories and origami:

Kallevig, Christine Petrell, 1993, *All About Pockets: Storytime Activities for Early Childhood*, p. 40, Broadview Hts., OH: Storytime Ink Intl.

Kallevig, Christine Petrell, 1993, *Bible Folding Stories: Old Testament Stories and Paper folding Together As One*, Broadview Hts., OH: Storytime Ink Intl.

Kallevig, Christine Petrell, 1991, *Folding Stories: Storytelling and Origami Together As One*, Broadview Hts., OH: Storytime Ink Intl.

Kallevig, Christine Petrell, 1992, *Holiday Folding Stories: Storytelling and Origami Together For Holiday Fun*, Broadview Hts., OH: Storytime Ink Intl.

Kallevig, Christine Petrell, 2001, *Fold-Along Stories: Quick & Easy Origami Tales For Beginners*, Cleveland, OH: Storytime Ink Intl.

Murry and Rigney, 1928, *Paper Folding For Beginners*, Dover.

Pellowski, Anne, 1987, *Family Storytelling Handbook*, p. 74-84 (two stories written by Gay Merrill Gross), New York, NY: Macmillan Pub. Co.

Schimmel, Nancy, 1982, *Just Enough To Make A Story: A Sourcebook For Storytellers*, p. 20-32, Berkeley, CA: Sisters' Choice Press.

Index

Storigami author, Christine Petrell Kallevig, is available to tell stories or present educational workshops at schools, conferences, conventions, festivals, or other gatherings. For details, visit foldalong.home.att.net or contact the publisher, Storytime Ink International at P. O. Box 470505, Cleveland, Ohio 44147.